LITTLE FISH

RAMSEY BEYER

LITTLE FISH

A MEMOIR FROM A DIFFERENT KIND OF YEAR

ZEST BOOKS

35 Stillman Street, Suite 121
San Francisco, CA 94107
www.zestbooks.net

Young Adult Nonfiction / Biography & Autobiography / Art
Library of Congress control number: 2013932098
ISBN: 978-1-936976-18-8
Cover and interior design: Ramsey Beyer

Manufactured in the U.S.A.
DOC 10 9 8 7 6 5 4 3 2 1
4500423066

Connect with Zest!
zestbooks.net/blog
zestbooks.net/contests
twitter.com/ZestBooks
facebook.com/ZestBook
facebook.com/BookswithaTwist
pinterest.com/ZestBooks

This book is for my parents, who gave me every opportunity they could, and for Daniel, who showed me how to care about things.

INTRODUCTION

Wait, wait. Don't get me wrong.
I really loved my life in Paw Paw.
But as a teenager who was into art and punk,
I wanted nothing more than to move to a place with "culture."
I glorified city-living.

So this is the story about how I made the leap, packed up my life, and moved to Baltimore-
re-enactment
mixed in with the awkward college freshman experience.
embarrassing content
Luckily, I documented my life long before I started making comics.
what would I do without you, livejournal?
9/12/03
hi. today was a very good day.
these are the reasons why:
i had my first 6 hour class. it wasn't horrible. it was my drawing class. it was actually kind of fun.
my new computer came in the mail and i'm now all hooked up. very exciting. it felt like Christmas.
i finished my self-portrait painting. now only one more self-portrait and two more drawings to go before my homework is done.
we hung out with two guys that i have seen around and have been wanting to meet and get to know since i've been here. they are very nice cool guys that i have lots in common with which makes me very excited.
we hung out very late and all ignored the fact that we have lots of homework.
tomorrow is my day off. i have training for work at 3. but it's still a day off from classes.
I actually wrote these pages when I was 18!
any page that looks like this is taken straight from the online journal i actually wrote when i was in my freshman year of college!

i had a weird habit of writing lists for a long time. i kept them in notebooks, but eventually used them to make my first zine! a zine is a cut-and-paste independent "magazine" that is filled with whatever you want!

all of the pages that look similar to this are pages from the first few issues of my zine, List. I also wrote a bunch of new list pages for this book.

And of course, I draw comics – so there are a lot of those, too.

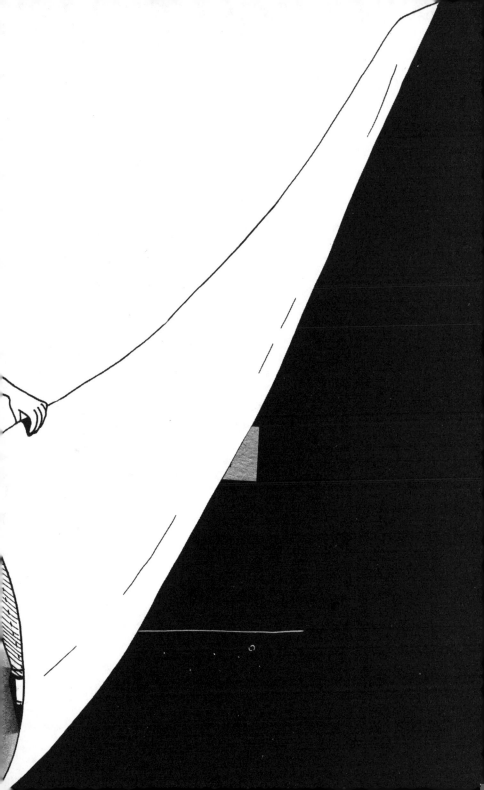

who i am

hi.

i am a: quiet, open, fun,
loud, quirky, artsy, happy,
bouncy, intelligent, excited,
dorky, laughy, lovey, young
but old, innocent, shy, laid
back, dedicated, opinionated,
18-year-old girl from
michigan that really
likes to make lists.

that is what this is.
        this is   me.
    and maybe you.

    if you ever want to really
know someone very quickly, ask
    them to make a list.

i make lists about everything.

    some of these are really old,
some are new, some i'll make up
        as we go.

Self-Portrait (In a nutshell)

THE BASICS

--i grew up in a small town in michigan
--i have two brothers and two sisters

--i play guitar in a band with my three best friends

--i like punk and indie music
--but i play in a pop band

--i've always wanted to live in a city

--i have really supportive parents who encouraged
  me to go to art school (which i know im really
  lucky for!)
--i have really supportive teachers

--i'm generally a happy person. things just don't
  really get to me. that's my favorite thing
  about myself

--i like to spend my time:
        -painting/drawing
        -playing on my hockey team
        -going out on the lake with friends
        -having bonfires
        -writing lists (which i've written in my
         journal for a really long time)
        -chatting online with cute indie boys from cities
        -driving around aimlessly singing along to music
        -hanging out with my family
     (even though they can drive me crazy, too)

-- it's almost time to go to college. i feel ready and excited,
   but like a little kid at the same time.

things i identify with:

punk - i got into punk when i was
14. i went through all sorts
of phases of punk but mostly
listen to indie and emo stuff.
it doesnt really sound "punk"
necessarily, but has punk and
diy influences and ethics. i
like all sorts of kinds of
punk music, though. except for
hardcore.xXX/ i hate hardcore!

straightedge - ok, so i dont really
call myself straightedge
because it makes me think
of macho hardcore dudes,
but i dont drink or do
drugs and dont think i ever
will. i definitely identify
with the straightedge ethos
but dont want to be lumped
in with those guys.

artxxxxx - so i dont really call
myself an "artist" because
i dont think i'm good enough
yet, but i've wanted to be one
since i was really young and
i hope to call myself one
one day.

country life - as much as i fight it,
rural life is in my blood.
even though i cant wait to
live in a city, i know that when
i'm older and settled, i will
definitely want to come back and
live on a farm.

ways to annoy me

-talk very loudly just to
call attention to yourself

-put on an act in front of
people

-talk a lot while i'm trying
to concentrate

-be hardheaded

-be two-faced

-sing loudly often

-constantly try hard to be
different/the same

-change the subject when you're
losing an argument

top 10 worst sounds

1) chewing really loudly
2) the sound of macaroni and
   cheese being stirred
3) when vine charcoal hits the
   paper wrong and makes a
   scraping sound
4) when you do a hockey stop
   the wrong way and your
   skates chatter
5) the sound of a group of
   people laughing when you're sad
6) someone playing drums when
   you're trying to focus (ie. tune
   your guitar)
7) the sound of people whispering
   and laughing
8) anyone doing anything when you're
   dead tired
9) chewing on ice
10) when you can't stop focusing on
    every little sound around you
    and they all build into a mass
    of overwhelming sounds

My Family

mom

My mom is a writer and does marketing for nonprofits. She is logical and to the point. She likes reading and stand-up comedy.
(I live with her now.)

My dad is a surgeon, but also has a lot of hobbies - like farming and flying airplanes. He's really goofy and likes to kid around. He wasn't around much when I was young because of his demanding career. (I lived in his house until I was 16, when my parents divorced.)

dad

rachel

My oldest sister is starting her adult life. She's 24 and wants to stick around Paw Paw and raise a family.

rosemary

My second oldest sister is 22 and finishing college. She's applying to law school and wants to stay in Michigan, or maybe live in Chicago. We shared a bedroom our whole lives until I was 16 and she went away to college.

My older brother is 20 and going to college for psychology. He plays hockey. We hung out a lot in high school and he dated my best friend Erin for a few years.

abe

graham

My younger brother is 16 and a sophomore in high school. He's into similar music as me and we get along pretty well. We've always been pretty good friends.

my family is:

-always supportive. i've
wanted to be an artist since
i was a kid and that was never
questioned.

-complicated. my parents divorced,
two years ago and im still trying
to figure out what type of
relationship ill have with each
of them.

-large. i have two brothers and
two sisters so family time is
hectic and busy.

    -midwestern

-liberal

-well-off, or at least my dad is.
im really lucky to have lived such
a comfortable life and have had
things handed to me for so long. i
try not to take that for granted.

-athiestic. i was raised without
religion and i know that has
played a large role in shaping me.

    -civil. we all get along
        reasonably well, all
            things considered.

GOING TO ART SCHOOL INSTEAD OF
A REGULAR UNIVERSITY

pros

-ive always wanted to
be an artist

-it would be filled with
other weirdos and punks
and creative types

-i wouldnt have to take
a lot of prerequisites
that im not interested in

-i might get good awards
and scholarships since i've
already taken so many art
courses

-it would push me to really
try hard at the thing that
i love most

-i feel like i would belong
there

-i'll be intellectually
stimulated and be able to
engage in conversation
with my peers about all
sorts of things from
contemporary art, to film
to music

-i wont have to take a science
or math class!

cons

-i might not be good
enough

-it might make me feel
burnt out and not like
art anymore

-who knows if i'll be able
to make a living as an
artist? maybe i'll have
to work a bad day job
my whole life even
though i have a degree

-i might not feel
well rounded or
academically stimulated

-in a nonart setting
everyone thinks im
really good at art.
at art school, i
would just be
average.

-there will be a lot
of pretentious art
kids and people trying
to shove their ideas
down my throat

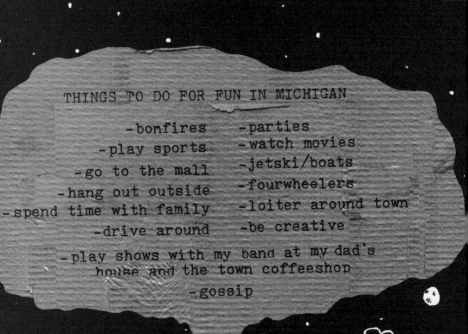

THINGS TO DO FOR FUN IN MICHIGAN

-bonfires   -parties
-play sports   -watch movies
-go to the mall   -jetski/boats
-hang out outside -fourwheelers
-spend time with family -loiter around town
-drive around   -be creative

-play shows with my band at my dad's
house and the town coffeeshop
-gossip

childhood.

grapes
  big white house
spiral stairs
   checkered kitchen floor
scary wine cellar basements
   french doors
      great dane
  houses made of hay
     forbidden lofts in big red barns
pear trees
     old ralph
         turtle sandbox

    wrestling with brothers
   "running away" into cornfields
man-eating swamp
 deer
  paddle boats
   sandbar
 finding clay in the lake
  family trips to 42 states
 airplane rides
   nerf guns
 building bridges

my oldest and best friends:

Merry

Merry and I became best friends after being in the same 3rd grade class. We were inseparable. We were together so often that people often asked if we were twins or sisters. Merry and I played on the same hockey team and did pretty much everything else together, too!

Katie was in my kindergarten class, but we really became friends because she lived a few doors down from Merry her whole life and was already best friends with her. katie is tough and sporty and, if we're being honest, kind of a bully - at least when we were little. Katie also writes music. Akkxf!

Katie

Frances moved to our town in 4th grade and lived down the street from Merry and Katie. She grew up in Florida and was sort of a tomboy, so she fit right in with our crew. She's really funny and sort of a klutz.

Erin started going to our school in 8th grade but lived a few towns over. Our town was part of a 'schools of choice' program, which meant that you could choose to go there even if you were out of the district. Erin is funny and sweet and was willing to go on weird adventures with us and learn drums to play in a band with me, Merry and Katie. We played in an all-girl pop band called Forever in Secret for four years!

These are my favorite people ever. I'm so glad I grew up with them, but I'm not sure how it will be once we're all separated. People say you don't stay friends with the friends you had in high school but I know I will.

ways my life might be different
     from other teens:

-i live on a vineyard and cornfield
-i got my boaters license when i was 12
-a large majority of male friends are
active hunters

-almost everyone i know lives on a lake
-i drive an hour and a half three days a
  week just to play on a girls travel
  hockey team

-i know how to weld because my friend
ryan works at an autoshop and taught
  me for an art project

-i play guitar in a band with my three
  best girlfriends and we set up house
  shows in my small town.

-i grew up on 100 acres of land and
spent most of my childhood outside
romping around in nature

-i'm not interested in dating at all.
 i have so many good friends and i don't
 want to make things complicated. i
  like not having to worry about that
   stuff (also maybe i'm totally scared
 of boys because i'm shy)

-i obsessively document my life on my
online journal and in lists. i'm an
 open book really.

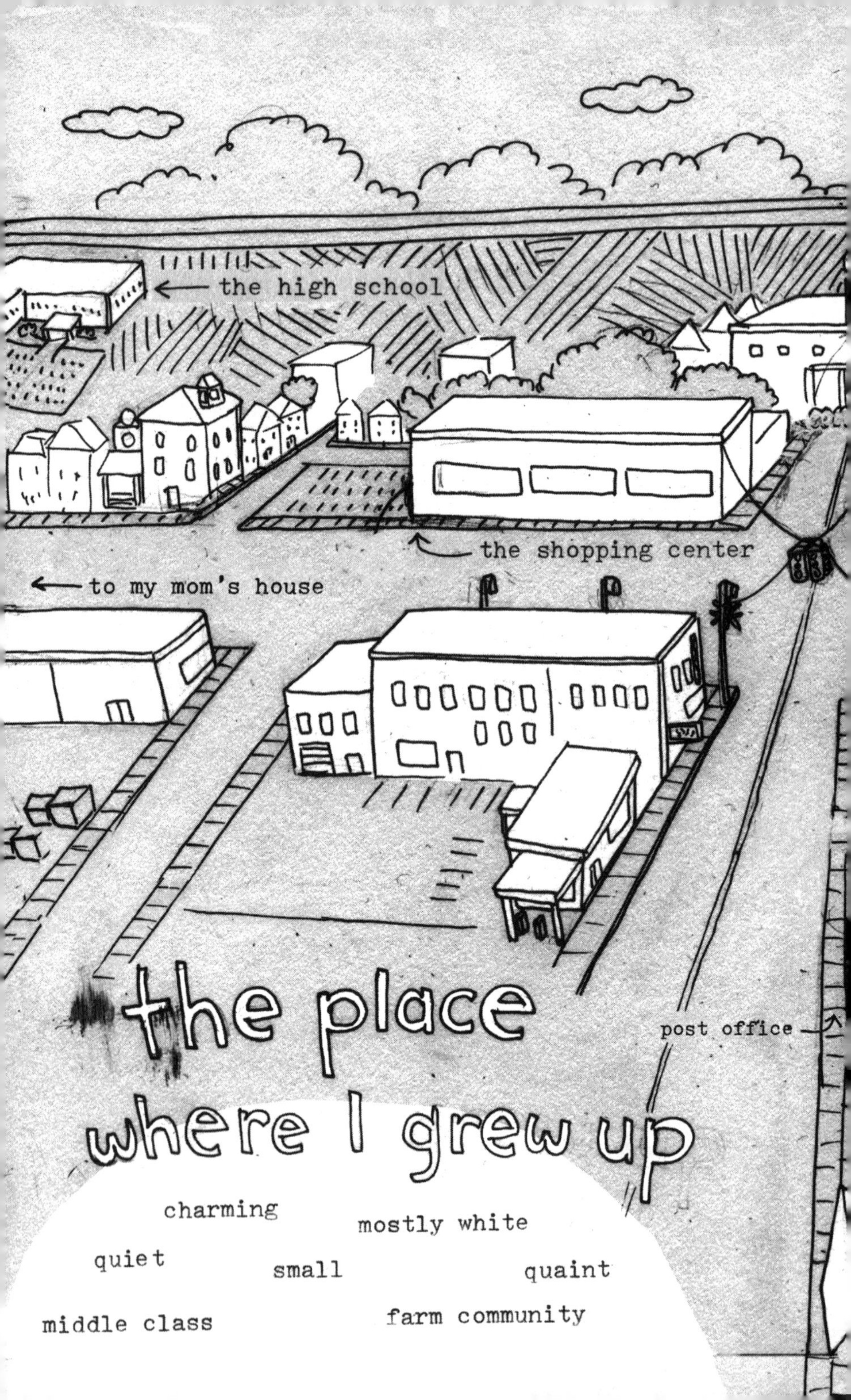

the high school ←

← to my mom's house

the shopping center

post office →

the place
where I grew up

charming

mostly white

quiet

small

quaint

middle class

farm community

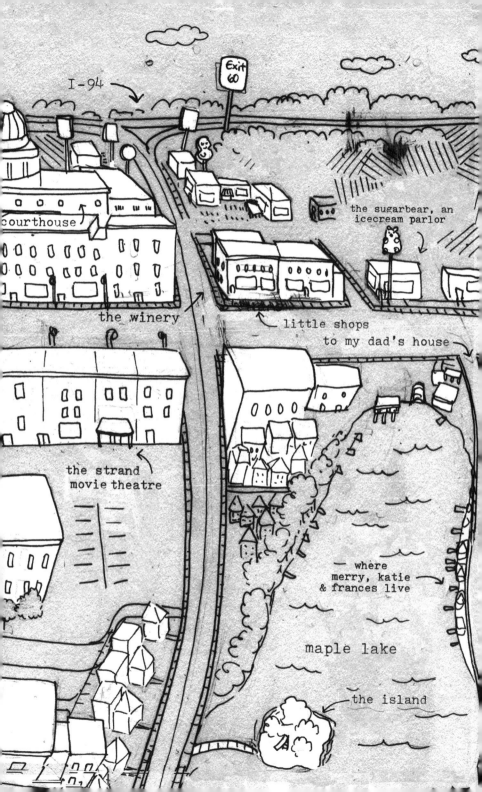

MERRY'S BASEMENT

-lots of super nintendo

-board games that we all get enthused about

--all cleaning the basement together, to music,
    because we spend so much time down there

-country music

-playing pool

-laughing a lot and being hyper

-picture taking

-wrestling and rough-housing like you
    only do with friends you've known forever

-people piled on the futons

-breaking things on accident, like
    the ceiling tiles. whoops?

-best friends and falling right
    back into place

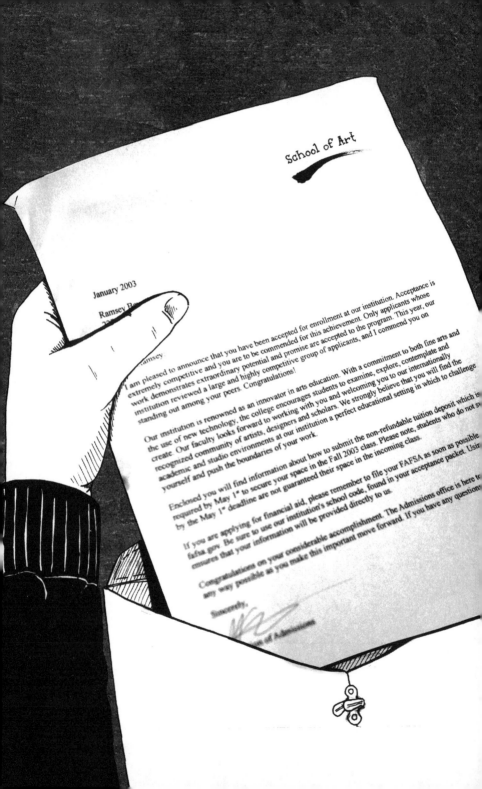

THINGS I'VE DONE TO PREPARE

(for college)

-worked hard in school for pretty much
as long as i can remember. im kind of
a goody goody.

-painted all day and night with my free time
(when i wasnt playing on my hockey team or
playing music with my best friends in a band)

-went to an extracurricular art academy after
school and on weekends to get even better at
drawing - i also went to art summer camp
for two summers in high school.

-talked to my friends a lot about where we will
all go and what kind of programs we want to find.

-visited a few schools. i narrowed down the
cities i wanted to live in first and then
picked my top three based on how good their
art schools were.

-after seeing the schools it was easier to choose.
i liked the one with the best 'campus' vibe.
i picked the school in baltimore because it was
high ranked, and had lots of grass and charming bricks.
baltimore had a cool art and music scene, and the
school offered me a lot of scholarships.

-got in touch with my new roommates after the school
sent me their info this summer. we've been writing
emails already!

-got ready to say good-bye to everyone and had the best
summer ever. i even met a boy right before i left,
so i had a fun summer fling before moving, too!

-packed everything up and rented a truck to
drive 600 miles away.

THINGS I'M MISSING HERE:

-broader perspective

-arts and culture

-diversity

-job opportunities

-opportunities for new relationships.
 i've known everyone here for so long.

-the chance to be anonymous or totally
 change who i am without everyone
 making a big deal out of it

-challenge. i never have to question
 myself here.

-museums, galleries, concerts

-room for growth

ways that college might change me:

-i might become a pretentious snob

-i might come back and think my
town and former life are too boring

-i might end up worrying about money
all the time - the typical"starving
artist"

-i might realize all sorts of things about
my town and realize i was more small-
minded than i even knew

-i might become a know-it-all
-i might realize i hate art if i'm forced
to do it for homework or deadlines

-i might end up doing a totally different
kind of art - like sculpture or performance
art or something weird like that. we have
to try all different things during
foundation year

-i might become a city-slicker like my
friend dan already teases me about being

things I can't wait for

-living in the city for the first time

-being on my own and figuring everything out as it comes my way

-living with roommates. I hope they're cool and I'm not stuck with anyone really annoying! and I hope they like me, too...

-finding some sort of diy punk and indie scene and getting to see bands play a lot

-my classes and learning new things. my classes sound intimidating but super interesting and fun.

-being closer to an ocean and being on the East Coast near lots of other cities

-riding public transit! Whenever I think of city life, this is the first thing that comes to mind. I hope I can find my way around.

-trying to make new friends and making myself be outgoing. I never realized how shy I felt until now, when I'm pushed outside of my comfort zone

-all the new art I'm going to make and the ways I'll be pushed creatively

-change of pace and change of perspective

THINGS I DO WITH
MY DAD:
- go out to dinner
- go to hockey practice/games
- watch movies
- work in his office
- get support
- visit college campuses to
  decide where to go to
  school

THINGS I DO WITH
MY MOM:
- spend time at home
- talk about life
- watch tv/movies
- go to hockey practice/games
- make dinner
- stuff around the house
- get support
- drive 600 miles to move
  away to college

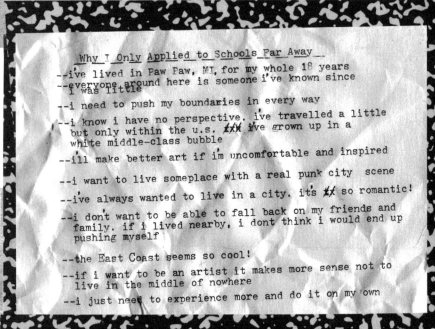

Why I Only Applied to Schools Far Away

--i've lived in Paw Paw, MI, for my whole 18 years
--everyone around here is someone i've known since
  i was little

--i need to push my boundaries in every way

--i know i have no perspective. ive travelled a little
  but only within the u.s. i've grown up in a
  white middle-class bubble

--ill make better art if im uncomfortable and inspired

--i want to live someplace with a real punk city scene

--i've always wanted to live in a city. it's so romantic!

--i dont want to be able to fall back on my friends and
  family. if i lived nearby, i dont think i would end up
  pushing myself

--the East Coast seems so cool!

--if i want to be an artist it makes more sense not to
  live in the middle of nowhere

--i just need to experience more and do it on my own

update from college? yeah.   8/23/03

we're top floor of an amazing house. brownstone style. all city and sweet. we have a balcony. we have a little quiet cute street right in the middle of everything. this isn't what college is normally like. is it? i thought i was supposed to have a prison cell dorm. i'm not complaining. the whole campus is amazing. all red brick and old historic buildings like a train station and a hospital restored into art studios, etc. i've only been gone two days and all i can think about is how i feel like i haven't talked to my best friends in so long. but. this place is soo amazing. beautiful. my apartment is huge. i'm lucky.

        so what have we been up to? lots of orientation stuff. we broke into little groups. we played games and got to know each other. thursday is a get-things-done day; get a bank account. get work study assignments. get your student id, etc. at night there are more games and question-and-answer sessions. from 10-12 there is a movie out on the grass on a big screen in the commons courtyard. Tomorrow, Sunday, and monday are three more full days of things like this. monday is a free trip to DC, so i'll probably go. Classes start Tuesday, the 26th.

Olivia is my roommate. We share the double room in the apartment. She's a vegan and gay rights activist from Peru. She came here to be a film-maker.

Katya is my housemate. She lives in the single room in our apartment. She's a Russian New Yorker who came here to be a painter.

Cory was in my roommate's orientation group and became one of our first friends outside of the house. He's from a small town in Rhode Island. He makes electronic music and came here to be a painter.

Nathalie lives in the apartment below us in the same rowhouse. She's a gamer from Miami who came here to be a graphic designer.

the way things have always been

- very rural

- routine, the same people and places for
  the entire first 18 years of my life

- comfortable, but fun

- comfortable, but boring

- supportive - i always had teachers, family
  and friends to help me along the way

- my four best friends around for every adventure
  since i was five years old

- very white and middle class

- quiet and quaint

- so small that we only had two stoplights in
  our whole town
- safe

- confining, i need to explore!
- easy

the way things are now

-very urban, in all the good and bad ways

-different, every day is something new
that i have to figure out! how to use
public transit, how to get to class,
how to get around safely at night...
how to make friends? i haven't had to
make new friends since i was little

-a little scary, i never really realized
how shy i was until i left my comfort zone

-very diverse, i definitely have some learning to do

-our college campus has more stoplights
than my whole town did

-limitless, i feel like i'm challenging
everything i thought i knew

-lonely... making new friends is weird.
i'm glad i went to orientation activities
so i know at least a few people

-did i say scary yet?

early

days

campus
map

Ways to try
make new friends:

.talk to people in class
.look friendly, but mysteriously cool...
            or something like that

.participate in campus activities. It seems
a little nerdy but I've already met a lot of
people that way in the first week.

  .join school clubs?

  .invite people over. have homework parties.

.remember that everyone else is in the same boat.
We're all little fish around here, not just me.
  Other people are probably nervous, too.

How do I even begin to
make new friends?
(I haven't had to do this since
I was a little kid)

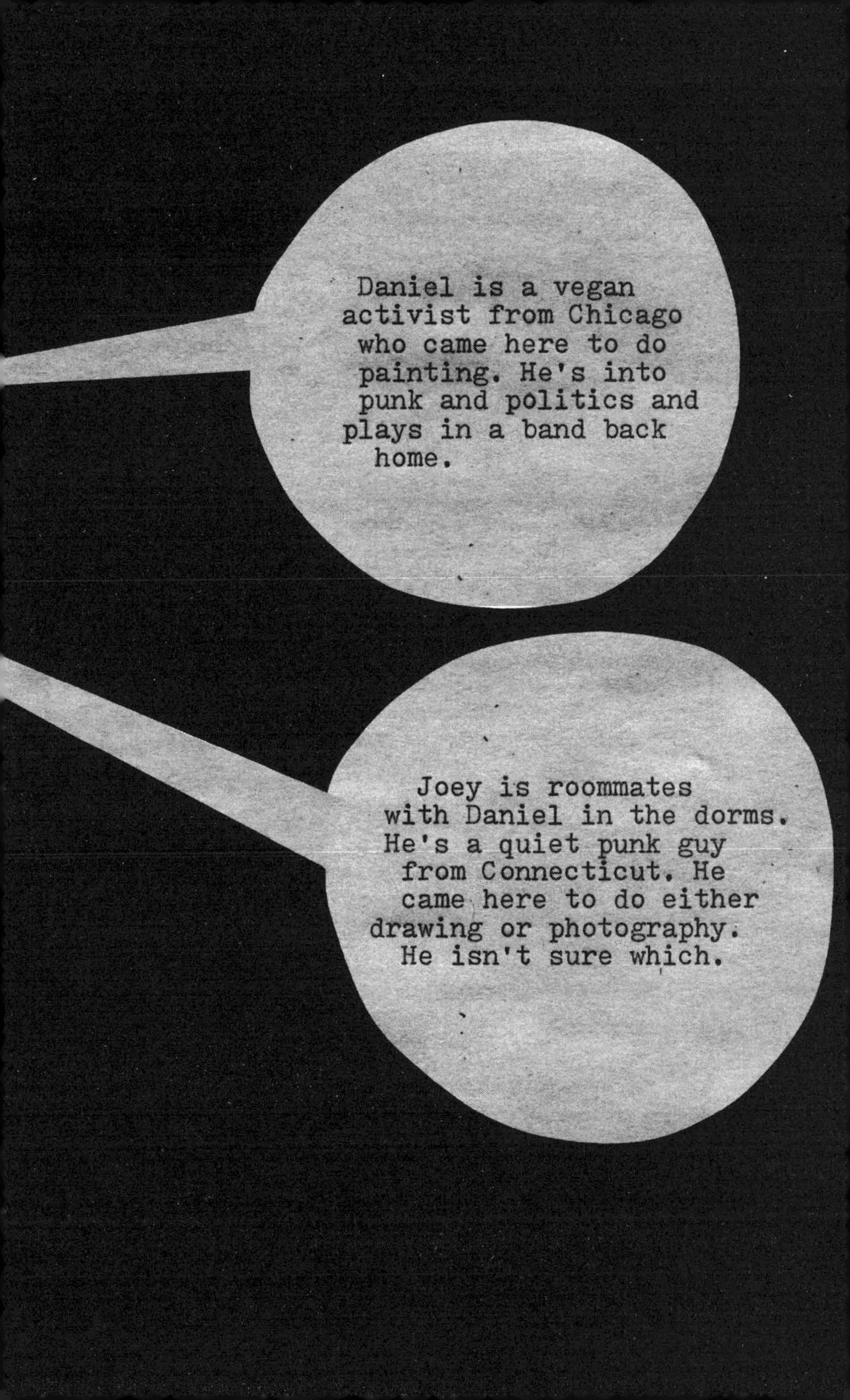

Daniel is a vegan
activist from Chicago
who came here to do
painting. He's into
punk and politics and
plays in a band back
   home.

Joey is roommates
with Daniel in the dorms.
He's a quiet punk guy
from Connecticut. He
came here to do either
drawing or photography.
He isn't sure which.

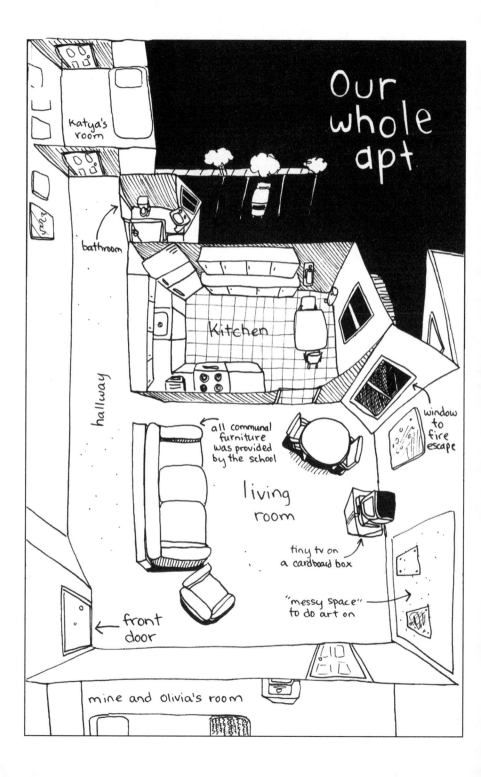

things that are underrated
. . . .

x burlap

x the color brown

x applesauce

x photobooths

x twine

x homemade paper

x new years eve

x the great lakes

x going sockless

x sleeping together with people
     on little beds

x dr. mario

8/30/03

today is when things got really interesting.

i got my schedule:

← yep!
a 6-hour class

monday = painting studio - 4pm to 10 pm.

tuesday = visual thinking - 8:30am to 12:30. and
art history - 1:30 to 4:15.

I hear this is
easy to test
out of so
I'm gonna try in a
few days
→ wednesday = digital media and culture - 8:30am to 2:00, and
academic writing workshop - 2:30 to 3:45

Another 6-hour class!
I hear this teacher is
killer and insults work
pretty harshly. so at
least I'm prepared for
that...

thursday = drawing 1 studio - 9am to 3pm

friday = off!

we've been informed that we do about 48 hours of homework a week. mostly art obviously. but, of course, it also
just depends on how hard you work. but yeah. i think i
can handle it. i hope.

9/12/03

hi. today was a very good day.
these are the reasons why:

i had my first 6-hour class. it wasn't horrible. it was my
drawing class. it was actually kind of fun.
my new computer came in the mail and I'm now all
hooked up. very exciting. it felt like Christmas.

i finished my self-portrait painting. now only one more
self-portrait, and two more drawings to go before my
homework is done.

tomorrow is my day off. I have training for work at 3.
but it's still a day off from class.

Hey!

Oh! Hey.

Weird. It's those punk boys from my digital class.

Hey.

Rams, this is Joey and Dan.

We're talking about animal rights, direct action versus passive action.
Dan is vegan, too.
Ahhh... makes sense.
What does?
Why you invited them over. You're such a vegan warrior.
It's Daniel, actually.
HA HA HA
You say that like it's a bad thing.

school is hard   sink or swim

-my very first assignment in drawing
class was to draw 100 hands and
100 feet by the following week,
thats a lot of drawing (!!) and that
was only one class out of four that
i had for homework that week

-my studio classes are 6 hours long.
with that and hours of homework for
each class, most of our socializing
is done while we work on homework at
the same time

-i have to defend myself in critiques
almost every day. its making me have
to think about every decision i make
for my art because i know i'll have
to back them up. obviously, this is
really good to do but its a little
scary. i never realized how shy i
was before, and i also realized that
ive never really been challenged or
backed into a corner fox i really
did exist as a big fish in a small
pond. i sort of could do whatever i
wanted without being questioned.

-ive already had a few all-nighters
and we're only a few weeks in. i guess
i'll learn time management pretty fast.

-that/ everyone talks about how they
try to weed kids out in the beginning
so only the really dedicated hardworkers
are left. i just have to remind myself of
that.

XXXXXXthings that scare meXXXX

nighttime alone

answering phones in
admissions

feelings

intimidating teachers

mice (though i never thought they did,
before here)

irrational people
tempers

falling

being startled
most roller coasters

deadlines

commitment
icy sidewalks

a lot of machines

things in the ocean

9/20/03

i dont know why, but i feel disconnected in a way —
from home, i guess. like i haven't really talked to many
of my best friends lately, and today i was thinking about
how no matter what, i'm going to be forgotten.

not forgotten totally, i'm just being dramatic... but,
you know, pretty soon people aren't going to think
about me, because that's what always happens. it
happens to me with people. after they leave, i just get
used to the fact that they're gone and i don't think
about them every day anymore. i've never had to be
the forgotten one, though, so it makes me kind of sad.
i guess i just woke up kind of sad. my mood fluctuates
a lot for no reason these days.
the weeks here go so fast for me so it feels like i'll be
home in no time, but at the same time, it's dragging on
forever! i'm counting down the days.
i really need to go do homework. i've been hanging out
way too much.

i miss my friends and home so much in the past few
days, and i don't know why, because i've been having a
lot of fun.

        reminder to myself.
    ramsey, allow yourself to be happy.
      do these things.
-------- -------   ---------------

.stop trying to understand/analyze
 people. you will understand them
 less in the end.

.dont procrastinate when it comes to
 people you really love.

.remember that you used to have to try
 to be sad. try to get that happy again

.dont selectively remember. remember the
bad with the good and appreciate life youve
lived for what it is, even the bad parts.

.dont forget to sleep. no matter what d
says, sleep is necessary.

.learn to spell necessary

.love things like you used to. people used
to think you were amazing.

.dont have crushes on boys that:
        .are in a relationship
        .dont like you back
        .dont like relationships

.make more lists

xxxxxxxxxxxxxxx xxxxxxxxxxxxxxxxxxxxxxxxx

the top five things i like about my neighborhood

1. the trees lining the brick sidewalks are so old and strong
   that they've lifted up a lot of the bricks on the sidewalk
   so it's all twisted around and uprooted (also easy to trip on!)

2. the man that walks with a horse and a big cart of fruits
   and vegetables, it has bells on it that jingle and he sings out
   the names of the produce on his cart when he walks by. with the
   mix of the bells and the horse's hooves, it sounds really pretty

3. the man that sits across the street on a bench. he sits there
   every day at the same time and does crossword puzzles. he was
   displaced and had to move one bench over because the tropical
   storm that just happened blew a tree over onto his bench.

4. the lights at night make everything glow orange. night lights on
   bricks and trees are one of my favorite things, especially with
   the weird purple glow that baltimore has at night

5. everyone says hello. there is a southern hospitality here that
   doesnt really make sense for the east coast, but it's a
   charming, underdog of a city and i think that makes people
   feel a stronger sense of community

9/21/03

the key to happiness (is not being alone when you're lonely)

—woke up really early and did homework/went online
—met and talked to a boy named ben, our neighbor
—went to his house and shared songs with our computers.
—more homework + internet.
—got a call from daniel and joe asking to hang out.
—walked into the city with daniel, joey, katya, olivia, and nat.
—ate at a very good restaurant.
—decided on a whim to walk to inner harbor to see flood
   damage from the tropical storm we just had
—hid our takeout food in a lot so we didn't have to carry it.
—watched a street artist in the harbor.
—went into the grocery store for free samples.
—went to the record store and looked at cds for a long time.
—found a magazine I like, which I split the cost for with nat.
—walked back toward the city.
—saw fireworks going off over the harbor.
—went dumpster diving and found a brand-new coffee grinder.
—went to pick up our takeout food that we hid and it had
   slugs all over it and inside. it was so gross!
—parted our ways with the boys. i came home super tired and
   sore from walking so far.

and here i am listening to my new cd. nat is lying on my bed
reading the magazine we bought. olivia and anna are watching
a french movie about lesbians, katya is doing homework, and
here i am... i miss everything about home, but i really like it
here, and i really really like the friends i've been with for the
past week because they're all pretty amazing.

The new gang

-a run-down of the crew i've been
hanging out with most

Katya likes: cityscape
paintings, art history,
Russian literature, theory,
and good films. She has a
long-distance boyfriend who
she met at an art camp.
She's very sweet and
intelligent.

Olivia likes: activism, films, going
on dates, trying new food, and
veganism. She is firey and
opinionated but quick to admit
when she's wrong. She's a
hopeless romantic.

Nathalie likes: indie music,
video games, painting, blogging
and good design. She stays up
late playing games online. Nat
is always willing to hang out.

Daniel likes: punk and hardcore, painting, photography, riding his bike, teasing me, theory, protests and activism. He's kind of shy and awkward, in a cute way. He's very opinionated.

Joey likes: punk and indie, riding his bike, photography, being organized, and making really detailed drawings. He's very quiet, blushes easily, and changes his mind a lot.

Cory likes: playing video games, painting, eating pizza, World of Warcraft, and electronic music. He collects anything with yellow smiley faces on them. He's friendly to everyone.

clubs I'm in

KNITTING CLUB

one of our resident advisors started this club
so we all went during the second week of school
and just kept going back. it was one of our
first excuses to hang out every week before
we all knew each other very well

we started this club after we decided to have
a movie night every week. at first it was just
my roommates and me, and the 3201 boys, but
if we made it an official school club, we could
get money to buy snacks every week.

DDR CLUB --

nat and cory both discovered that they share
a love of video games. they play against
each other online from their respective dorms,
but they also both love Dance Dance Revolution,
so they bought the game. i had never played
it before, but it's pretty goofy and fun, so
we all play it in the common space at the dorms.

ZPOINT --

daniel and olivia started going to zpoint,
the political action club. they convinced me
to start going. it's a lot of discussion about
things i don't fully know about but it's
interesting and i'm gonna go to my first

small town
(and feeling self-conscious about it)

-realizing the lack of diversity in my life.
 i always thought i had a pretty diverse
 friend group, but i'm realizing that's just
 by small town standards.

-everyone here is ✗ political and has strong
 opinions about a lot of issues i've never
 really even paid attention to (or never even
 heard of...)

-i can talk about monet and picasso but don't
 know anything about serrano or rothko or
 jeanne claude and christo. my knowledge
 of art history is limited to all the most
 obvious people, and i have no contemporary art
 knowledge at all! i already feel behind and
 i just got here.

-i've been wearing my hair in braids since the
 7th grade and feel like i look like a little
 kid. i don't really have a style. kids here
 dress really well or really strange or
 sophisticated. i feel decidedly uncool.

10/28/03

i wish i could explain how i feel. i wish i even knew how
i feel.

being here is just weird sometimes. everything is
uncertain. i don't know how i feel. i don't know how
people feel about me. i don't know what people are
thinking. who really means something to me, who i
really matter to at all.

i guess i'm just used to knowing who really loves me
and who i wouldn't miss and who would be truly sad
if i wasn't around. my friends at home make me feel
happy when they text me with the words "come home."
i know they care. i know they miss me. i know they
like when i'm around and that they really know who i
am. i don't know that anyone here feels that way about me.

it takes time, i know. i'm just used to it always being
there.

i go through weird phases here. one week i'm happy
and loved and accepted and the next i'm just really
lonely and lost. i don't know where i am right now.

things we do for fun

-homework together, or draw each other
 in our sketchbooks

-have big movie nights

-listen to records at daniel, joey and cory's
-plan big birthday parties for each other
-play old nintendo games
-hang out on the roof

-walk around the city late at night
-ride bikes, now that i finally have one.
 i was really jealous that daniel and joey
   could cruise around and that i walked everywhere.

-go to campus parties
-late-night pizza (without cheese since olivia
and daniel are vegan)

-have big sleepovers where we stay up late and
 then push mine and olivia's beds together to
 make a giant bed we can all sleep on.

-have debates and political conversations.

-tell stories about our homes, or high school.
 turns out most people didn't like high school?
 i loved it! i realize more every day how
 easy i've had it in my life so far, i'm very lucky.

-go see bands play at the art space or the talking
head or the ottobar

My hair is too poofy. That's why I wear braids every day.
They take no effort.
I like your braids. They're cute.
thanks.
Your hair isn't normally black, is it?
Nope. It's blond. I dyed it right before coming to school.
and yes, I know how cliché it is to dye your hair black before going to art school.
You wanted a fresh start. Totally normal.
I almost decided to start going by my middle name. No one would even know.

words i hate

- creamy
- chunky
- cunt
- tummy
- panties
- dong
- snog
- squish
- snuggle
- crotch
- cuddle
- squash
- fuck (in context of sex)
- giggle
- nose
- snot
- sellout
- poser
- gay (used out of context)
- taint
- cod
- queef
- twat

ew.

11/17/03

this weekend consisted of:

.giving a 20-person tour for my workstudy
 job in the admissions office. i'm gonna
 leave this place as a really great public speaker!
.going to the presentation about the painting department.
 they give talks about each major that you can attend to
 meet instructors and upperclassmen to help you decide
 which major to choose. i know i'm going to be a painting
 major already.

.had a big hangout where we all straightened our hair.
 i have no idea why but we all decided to do it. we
 straightened mine, nat's, daniel, joey, cory, and our
 new friend ben's (he's our neighbor that we just met).
 it was really silly.

.falling asleep to the movie we were all watching.
.writing letters on my new typewriter
.not doing homework
.going thrifting and finding a bike!
.trying to fly a kite on the roof but failing
.hanging out and eating lots of chinese
.going to a masquerade ball. people made some elaborate
 masks! it is art school, after all.
.walking to the corner store at 1am to buy candy and pop
.taking the campus shuttle home so we didn't have to walk.
 it was conveniently sitting in the lot.
.sleeping in
.decorating my bedroom more
.writing another letter
.starting my drawing homework
.which ended up with a lot of people coming over for
 a homework party and hanging out for a long time
 while doing work.

and suddenly i have a big group of friends
again and i dont feel so lonely...

**ALL IN A BRIEF FIVE-MINUTE WALK
I WITNESSED THE FOLLOWING THINGS:**

--an inflatable nomadic shelter in front of our house being
  critiqued by a sculpture class

--the mystery boy that i see around and always wonder what
  he's thinking. not because i think he's cute but just
  because he looks mysterious!

--the crossword puzzle man that sits across the street
  from our house on a bench. he passed by me and said hello.
  i think he remembers that one day i stopped to talk to
  him, or maybe he just said hello because i smiled at him.

--a man suntanning in his backyard! it's funny to see people
  suntanning in the city. i don't know why. i've never thought
  about it as something you would do in a city i guess.

--four little boys hanging out by the dumpsters behind the
  elementary school insisting on me telling them my name, but
  trying to guess before i could even tell them. they kept
  guessing typical names and i warned them that they would
  never guess it. they thought it was really funny.

--lots of sunshine

fall

recent best feelings ever: 11/25/03

-painting in a house by myself at night
with music on loud

-lots of friends actually coming over every
wednesday to watch a bad teen drama tv show
together, just like i used to do every week
with my best friends in high school

-good critiques

-getting out of class early and suddenly
having more time than i know what to do with

-really good new friendships

-warm windy fall days

-remembering that i'm at one of the best art
schools in the country and remembering to feel
really grateful for it

-getting mail

-really good meals with friends

-thoughts of home

-listening to bands i used to listen to and being
reminded of really warm memories

things i want to have happen during
fall break at home

1. band practice
2. hear katie's new songs!
3. eat at kliens, one of my favorite places
4. go ice skating
5. sew some jackets so they fit me better
6. do laundry
7. hear frances's story about her
   roomate and her razor

8. hang out with my friends!
9. sleepovers
10. girls night
11. see that boy who i had a summer crush on
12. buy film for my camera
13. have a family dinner
14. play with my dog! i always forget to miss him,
    but when i remember, it's a big bummer
15. bake cookies
16. make some presents for christmas
17. go to a show?
18. hang out with everyone all at once and
    stay up late and laugh a lot

weird things about being home

-i have a lot of new stories and friends, but i suddenly realized that all my high school friends have other new friends from college too and i won't be a part of that. that never really crossed my mind.

-having to drive everywhere, and worse, having to share the car with four siblings. i don't really have curfews and things like that so i didn't expect to feel like i would not have the freedom i have at college, but i ~~did~~ definitely am more limited here. i can't just do what i want. i sound like a whiny brat.

- noticing little things about my hometown that i never noticed before, like that people use weird sexist and subtly racist language... it used to just blow past me without much thought but now that we talk a lot about ~~the~~ feminist theory, gender politics, and race and privilege so much in school, it's really hard to ignore how internalized all of that stuff is here ~~it~~ (even how much of it was in me!)

good things about being home
~~things ive missed in michigan~~

-my parents

-my family dog

-being around people i'm totally comfortable with
-good meals cooked by my mom

-not having to stress about getting work done

-seeing people i haven't seen for too long. this is probably the longest i had gone without hanging out with my best friends, since i was like...five.

-seeing my summer crush and realizing it would be the last time we hung out, and that it felt ok

-missing my school friends - being home made me realize how close i'm starting to feel to certain people and i'm actually a little excited to get back

-sitting in front of the fireplace

-the first snow of the year

```
       things i want to have happen during
             fall break at home

1. band practice
2. hear katie's new songs!
3. eat at kliens, one of my favorite places
4. go ice skating
5. sew some jackets so they fit me better
6. do laundry
7. hear frances's story about her
   roomate and her razor

8. hang out with my friends!
9. sleepovers
10. girls night
11. see that boy who i had a summer crush on
12. buy film for my camera
13. have a family dinner
14. play with my dog! i always forget to miss him,
    but when i remember, it's a big bummer
15. bake cookies
16. make some presents for christmas
17.     go to a show?
18. hang out with everyone all at once and
    stay up late and laugh a lot
```

i'm so lucky to have such a good home life and such a good school life. i wish everyone did. it's weird how the instant i step off the plane, i'll be in a totally different universe/mind-set/routine.

i go from snow and farms and small towns, family and best friends in the entire universe, to crammed brick rowhouses and city, fall and sunshine and more best friends and being alone sometimes. I only have 3 weeks until i'm in michigan again for a whole month for winter break. 3 weeks goes by so fast and i'm glad for that.

i love (after a visit home)

november 28, 2003

:michigan
:snow
:the OC
:my dog, ;hunter;
:my family
:my house
:sleeping on the floor
:my amazing best friends
:dr. mario
:watching the 80-yr-old lady talk
    about sex on the oxygen channel
:new shoes
:snow! and lots of fun with it
:good conversation
:good music
:conan
:reading about happy friends
:pop machine races
:calling it pop instead of soda
:hearing katie's new song
:good food
:scarfs and mittens and hats
:happiness

things about baltimore i've grown to love.

-the sound of the lightrail at night

-tripping on bricks

-laughing kids at 8am and 3.30pm

-walking everywhere

-shows

-the lightrail

-being paranoid at night

-thai food

```
           longest work day
             12/3/03



    this is definitely one of the longest
days i've experienced at school so far.
straight work. no break.

-class from 8:30am - 10:30am (we got
 let out really early for some reason)

-worked on a painting until 12:30

-ate lunch

-class from 1:30 to 4pm (also let out
 a half hour early)

-worked on our art history presentation
 with my group from 4-6:30. we had to
 choose a cultural institution in the
 city of baltimore to study.

-dinner

-worked on my website for digital class
   from 7:30pm to 3:13am


  tomorrow means half of the week is done,
 which means only 2.5 weeks until i'm
 going home to michigan for an entire month.
```

Hey guys! I'm back. Look at these photos I just got developed. So cute.
PUSH
Holy cow, Katya.
GASP
Like it?
You had to have cut off like ten inches! I'm so jealous. One day.
You look so much older! Wow! So good.

Jeez. This already feels like so long ago, but we've only been here a few months.
Katya with really long hair! Already ancient history.
Oh my god, Rams - How about this one?
What? Which one?

i've been feeling all underwhelmed & blah & homesick & like i really need a break from this stuff. every-thing is just the same all the time and nothing exciting ever happens. but then i realized this:

i NEVER leave campus!!

this is not what i pictured college to be like. i was thinking about how everyone always says "welcome to the real world" when you graduate, but this is not the real world! this is an art-school bubble.

i don't know anyone outside of school. i rarely leave campus. i do go to the occasional show, but i always just go with kids from here, and i don't meet anyone new. i'm trapped. that's what it feels like. so when i start to feel like i'm going crazy with everyday life, that's when i start feeling homesick because home is something different.

i'm fine. i just need to remember to leeeeave campus sometimes and explore baltimore outside of a school context.

finals week

        -sleep deprivation, both from
    pulling all-nighters and from
    a final project where i stayed
up for 48 hours straight and
documented my appearance

-midnight breakfast provided by
my school

  -never not doing homework when
  we're all hanging out

  -visiting each other in studio
    buildings

-keeping each other awake and working

  -pushing boundaries

    -nerves and anxiety

      -bonding over exhaustion

-teachers bringing snacks around
  to the studios/labs in the middle
  of the night because they know
were all there working

  -wrapping up a semester's worth
    of hardwork

```
         things i'll miss
       about this semester

     -everyone being new and on
     a level playing field

     -my friends who are transferring
     and dropping out. they say they
     use foundation year as a way to
     weed people out and it seems
     to have been pretty successful


     -my digital class with daniel & JOey.
     at least i'll still have drawing II
     and now sculpture with Daniel


     -feeling totally fresh and new.
     i felt so wide-eyed when I first
     got here but now i really feel
     like i know the ropes. it's great
     to feel settled but it will
       definitely be more routine from
     now on


  -my painting professor. i decided to
  take an animation class for a big
  change of pace. i figure that's
  something i won't learn how to do
    anywhere else. might as well
       try it out.


       -being a little fish. it was
       scary but fun, too.
```

THE BEST THINGS ARE:

-going to sleep with the sound of your
 best friends all out in your living
 room laughing and having fun and being
 comfortable around each other, finally.

-carrying a couch up a flight of stairs
 and it making you and your friends laugh
 so hard you nearly drop it

-movie nights

-late night ice cream runs

-chinese food every single saturday from
 a chinese place called 'eat must be first'

-calls home to friends

-having a friend nickname my winter hat 'cloud'
 and people actually continuing to refer to it
 by name

-pop punk sing-alongs to bands we all listened
 to when we were 13

-laying around talking about nothing and growing
 closer

things i learned at my first
semester in art school: ~~xxx~~

-art school, as an idea, makes me feel
a little weird. sometimes it feels really
forced to churn out project after project
and expect to feel any sort of connection
with the work you're making. but i guess
that's just how foundation year works.

-concept is just as important, if not more,
than technique. i never push any conceptual
boundaries and need to

-critiques will make you more confident, but
also better at accepting criticism. it also
makes you think more about all the decisions you
make with your work because you know you will have
to defend them later.

-making friends takes a little time, but once you
do, it's so worth the effort.

-it only really takes a month or two before fresh
eyes wear off and everything starts to feel routine.
it's unreal that that can happen so quickly after
moving all the way across the country.

-i'm pretty mature and responsible compared to a lot
of people my age. some kids around here don't even
know how to do their own laundry...still! after a
whole semester.

-i've never been political or formed strong opinions
because i've never felt confident enough to defend
myself. i think that's starting to change... daniel
pointed out that ignorance is bliss is a pretty,
well...ignorant way to live. i had never really thought
about it before, but that's what i was choosing. i'm
smart enough to have strong opinions and defend myself.

-i've lived a very privileged life. i've lived
comfortably and have been supported and have had a lot
of opportunities and resources. it's real easy to take
all that for granted when it's just what you're used to.

-i think i'm afraid to have real feelings for anyone.

today is my second to last painting class. this semester is almost done. i'm very excited. yes, but i'll miss some things about this one. it's weird how much change occurs within one semester. i'll start the new semester at a very very different place from when i started the present one. i'm thinking of all the reasons things are different now from how they were then. and i'm deciding not to list them because maybe i let people be too aware of how i am on the inside. most people aren't like that. maybe i shouldn't be either.

today i walked far into the city alone. it was nice and lots of places reminded me of some places from home. i'm very relieved that i'm not as stressed as most kids here are about finals. somehow i managed to make my workload not so heavy. somehow i've managed to have a grasp on time management.

today is one of those days where i don't really know how i feel or if i feel anything at all.

12/15/03

daniel made me feel emotional
tonight. suddenly i felt jealous
out of no where, which is just . . .
weird. (?)

he went on a date with someone.

WINTER IN MICHIGAN

-comes in late October

    -is soft and white and sort
     of purple at night

-stays crisp and white

  -is something we have all learned
  to travel with. roads are plowed
   by the time you wake up in the
    morning and most people have snow
    tires

  - i have so many michigan snow
  memories, from tying sleds behind
  pickup trucks and getting pulled
  down the street to snowmobiling
  through the woods, to ice skating
  on the lake

    -feels like the time to just stay
     inside in front of the fireplace.
    it's always easy to not go anywhere
    in the winter in michigan, or when
     you do, you go in a heated car

    -feels warm and quiet, despite
     the cold

      -is something i look forward
        to every year

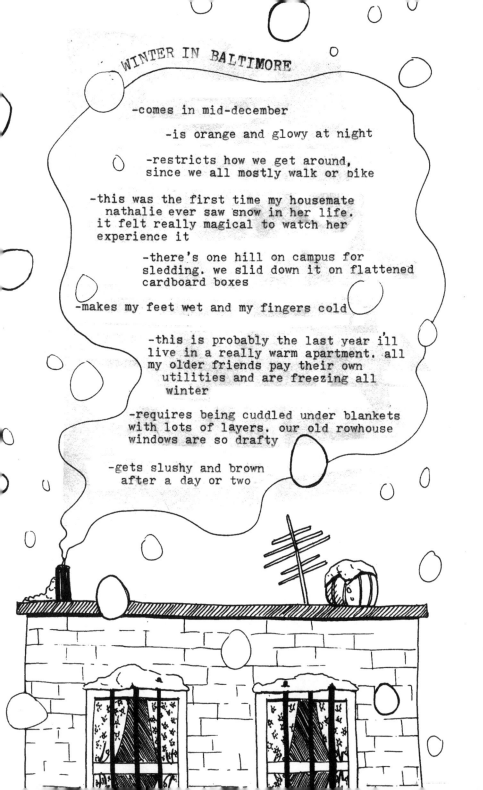

WINTER IN BALTIMORE

-comes in mid-december

-is orange and glowy at night

-restricts how we get around,
since we all mostly walk or bike

-this was the first time my housemate
nathalie ever saw snow in her life.
it felt really magical to watch her
experience it

-there's one hill on campus for
sledding. we slid down it on flattened
cardboard boxes

-makes my feet wet and my fingers cold

-this is probably the last year i'll
live in a really warm apartment. all
my older friends pay their own
utilities and are freezing all
winter

-requires being cuddled under blankets
with lots of layers. our old rowhouse
windows are so drafty

-gets slushy and brown
after a day or two

12/20/03

tonight was lots of fun. i'm really glad this is how i spent my last night before break.

things have been pretty good lately friendwise, i'll definitely miss everyone over break! a whole entire month without thrifting and 'eat must be first' and knitting club and record-listening parties and lying around talking about nothing.

tonight, nat, ben, daniel and i went to a house show. it was a birthday party. the bands were great. it made me like hardcore a little more. i think seeing bands play live makes me more into it. we met some people from the area that actually don't go to our school. there was a lot of candy and good food, since it was a party. we asked all these kids random questions to get to know people we didn't know. after the bands were done, we hung out for a while, and daniel tried to show us hardcore moves. it was really nice getting off campus.

tonight was fun.

i leave in 3 hrs for the airport. i will be home until january 20th! a whole month . . .

BYE
BYE
CYA RAMROD
Bye.
Cya Daniel.
Wait! Daniel.
Yeah?
You should give me a hug. I hug everyone else but I've never hugged you.
Oh.
Yeah, okay.

home
for the
holidays

z z

12/21/03

i'm home.. i'm glad.
BUT i already miss school
friends and it's only been two
days. i really need the best of
both worlds somehow.

yesterday included the following;
-my plane getting into detroit at 11;30
-being picked up by my dad and his wife
  and two of my siblings
-going to a vegetarian restaurant in
  ann arbor, the same one i had gone to
  with my summer crush. it made me a
  little sad that i wouldn't see him this
  visit, even though i hadn't thought about
  him since thanksgiving.
-driving home to paw paw, unpacking
-going to katie's to eat pizza and to
  bake a cake for erin's birthday
  and to just sit around
-going to erin's to give her the cake
  and sing her happy birthday and just
  hang out
-home to chat online with friends from
  school. it's weird that they all have
  different worlds to go back to too

the end of the year

- started out the year as a
  senior in high school
- got accepted to the schools i
  applied for
- did one last summer at art camp
  - spent the rest of the summer having
    fun with friends and making the most
    of the time we had left
  - packed up my things and moved across
    the country
- started college and campus life
- had ups and downs and awkward transitions
- learned a lot about myself
  - made an amazing new group of friends
- but felt lonely in the process
  - visited home and felt a new sense of
    appreciation for my family, home friends,
    nature and leisurely living
- felt sad about moving forward

- but felt ready to get back and see what's next
  - had an amazing new year's eve watching my
    friends' band play, going to an '80s-
    night party, and watching fireworks
    at midnight with people i love

1/2/04

So I've been thinking and this makes me sort of sad:

I could easily be happy if this was the only life I had, but I definitely could not if my school life was the only one I had. And it only makes me feel sad because I really love the friends I've made at school and they're amazing, but I think if I could logically find a good reason to stay home, I would. I'm glad I can't, though, because it's an experience I need. I remember constantly trying to convince myself of that when I had to leave for the first time: Still working on it...

(big)
  scars i have acquired:
''''''''''''''''''''''''''

moped exhaust pipe burn on the
back of my right leg --1995

1-in scar in the middle of my
chest from slipping while
climbing a fence with wet feet
after running through sprinklers
on a summer night -----2oo3

1-in scar on the inside of my right
wrist from walking through the
woods on rollerblades and tripping
on a stick (hey. i was in 3rd grade.)
           -----1993

hot-melt glue-gun burn on my left
thumb   -----2004

a total lack of faith in relationships
because of the end of my parents
marriage when i was 16 - an w/
emotional scar   -----2001

numerous scars on my arms and hands
from kittens with claws--1993-1994

scar on underside of my chin from
falling down and sliding on the
cement when i was being pulled
behind an adult tricycle on
rollerblades with a skirope.
  (once again, 3rd grade.)---1993

How's home? As hectic but boring as you had guessed? Or did it end up being kinda nice to be back?
Pretty much. My friends here are the best. But now I miss all of you instead. When is your band playing?
I'll be there! I'm stoked to see your band...even though it is hardcore.

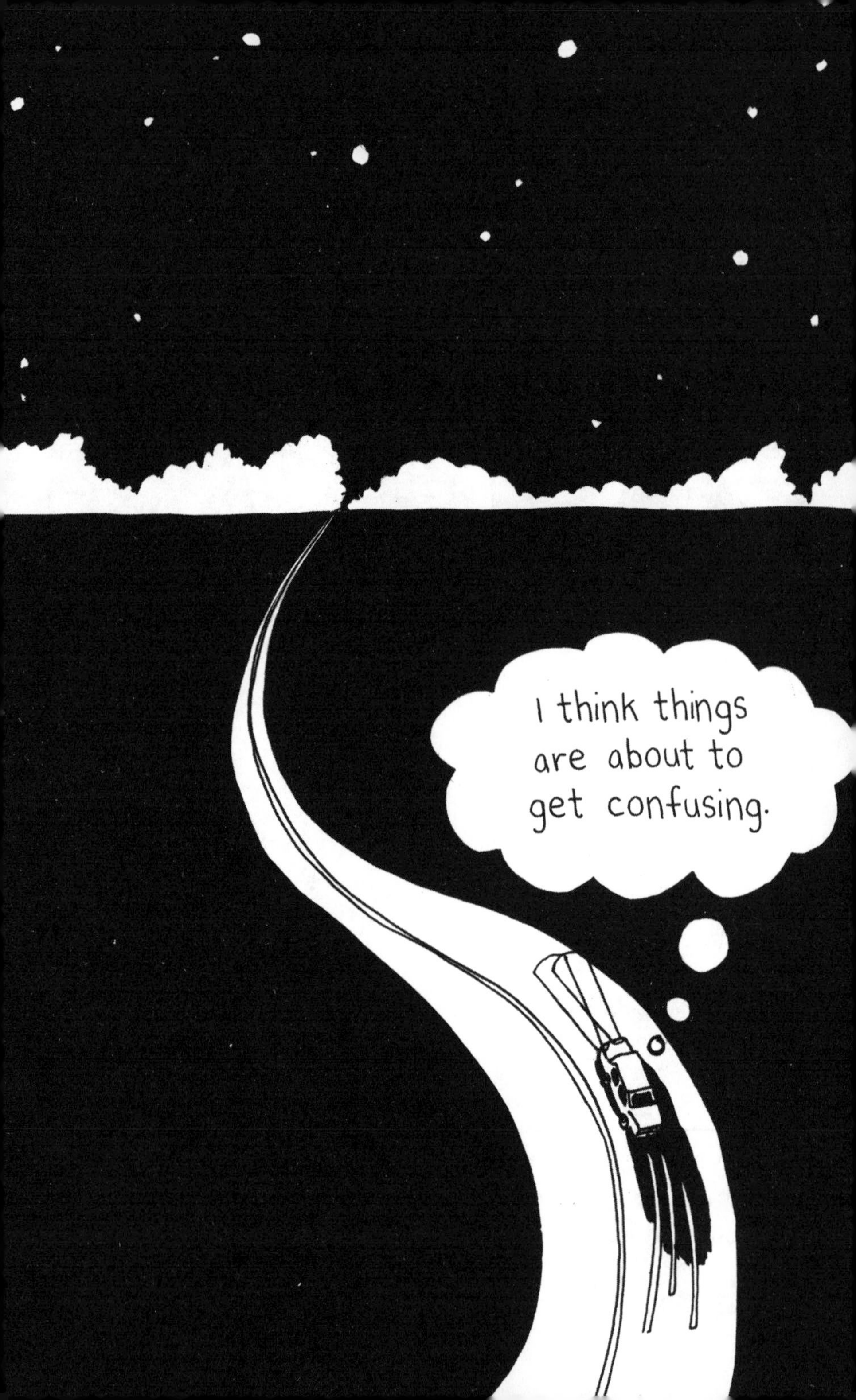
I think things are about to get confusing.

A NIGHT IN CHICAGO

—seeing new friends and introducing them to old ones

-sweaty basements filled with punk kids

-getting a glimpse into daniel's life at home and feeling like i know him better as a result

-long car rides singing along to our favorite songs

-getting to meet daniel's home friends and tag along to their hang out spots

-ears ringing from too loud music

-feeling especially conflicted about a sense of "home" and what it means and how it's made

-feeling alive with all sorts of feelings

1/3/04

last night was really fun. dominic, taylor and i went to chicago to see daniel's band play. it was warm and gloomy out and felt pretty perfect. it was really nice to see daniel again and it made me remember what i love about being at school and why it'll be okay to go back there and leave home once again. i was starting to forget and wish i could stay here forever. it came just at the right time.

top five reasons daniel is really cool:

1. hes just a nice boy. i know they say that nice guys finish last or whatever, but i think being a nice boy is a good thing.
2. he's socially awkward and it's kind of cute
3. hes passionate about things and encourages me to be
4. he likes good music sometimes and is making me like other types of music
5. i can talk to him like we're best friends... online at least

top five reasons i should cut off my braids
1. ⬛⬛ i've had them since the 8th grade.
2. they've become my identity and i don't want
    something so arbitrary to define me
3. i could have other cool looks, maybe?
4. i should try something new. take risks.
5. it makes people think i'm really innocent
    (yes, i AM really innocent, but people don't
    need to know that just by looking at me)

top five reasons i'll probably
never get rid of them

1. i'm afraid of change
2. people would make a big deal out of it
   and i don't like the attention
3. a lot of people really like them
4. ?
5. ? i guess this is more like a top three

top five things i need to accomplish when i
                           get back to school:
1. explore the city more
2. create a piece of art i feel passionate   about
3. write letters home
4. meet new people
5. go to the talking head club because i was told
   kids hang out there at night and it could be
   a good place to make non-school friends

1/15/04

Tomorrow is my last day and it will be a lot of fun because my friends and i always hang out all day right before I leave. I just hate that I have to have 'last days' because that, in itself, is not fun. It bums me out a lot to keep having little glimpses of home while I'm trying to create a new one. I hate leaving and get sad about it, but at the same time I'm excited about going. I guess that's how a lot of things in life are.

on the horizon...

-my 19th birthday, coming up fast

-trying new things. i'm taking an animation class!

-a new semester

-meeting new students who have transferred

-apartment hunting for next year

-continuing to develop friendships

-applying to be a counselor at the art camp i went to every summer

-continuing to try hard and work like crazy

-pushing myself and not settling

-figuring out how i feel and what i feel for people... and what to do about those feelings...

1/25/04

things have been good here. this really just feels like my life now. when i stop and realize that, it's very weird because at one point all i could think of was going home, and i kept comparing my friends here to my friends there, but now I've gotten so close to my friends here that they just feel like an equal alternative to home. that is a really great feeling. i remember all through middle school and high school i wished i could go to another school for at least a month just to see what starting over felt like and to see if i could actually make friends with people who didn't know me before we were even old enough to know how to judge. i guess college was the opportunity for me to take that chance, starting over, and I'm really glad i did.

we've been meeting more people this semester and it's fun. i think meeting new people and getting to know them might be my favorite thing. there is so much uncertainty and mystery. who knows if they'll turn out to be a really good friend or just an acquaintance. or maybe more

in other news, people keep begging me to cut my hair.

in a perfect relationship we would

february 1, 2004

.lay around playing video games

.walk at night

.wrestle
.feel content

.hold hands

.discuss

.tease
.have inside jokes

.cuddle

.learn new things

.have movie nights

.have sleepovers

.play board games

.take photobooth pictures

.trust

.ask each other questions

.try new things

.write each other notes

.be lazy together

.debate

times when you should take a hint:
february 3, 2004

.if my eyes start to wander, im probably
bored with what youre saying

.if i joke about having a crush on
you, i probably really do have a crush
on you

.if i give short answers and act like
im focusing intently on something else,
leave me alone

.if i act awkward when youre being touchy
feely or flirty, im not interested

.if were debating and im strong in my
opinion, it probably wont change because
of what you say

.if i say im sleepy or start yawning in an
overly obvious way, i probably want you to
go home

.if im cool with hugging you a lot, i reall
appreciate your existence

Little Things
2/5/04

-jumping up and down
-change
-inside jokes
-guilt-free lazy days
        -singing loudly
        -knowing looks
-windy days
-homemade tote bags
-good thrift store finds
-feeling okay with someone
-distorted mirrors
-music in headphones
-seeing genuine smiles
-holding hands
-photobooths
-home
-learning
-hugs
        -finishing something knitted
        -gifts that show you really
         know someone
        -rescuing little kids from
         headlocks
        -the way light looks on
         things at night
        -when people pick up on
         something small
        -lying in bed without
         sleeping
        -the smell of bouncy balls

things to be appreciated on a
_ ni̲gh̲t̲ li̲ke̲ tonight:̲ _ _ _ _ _

   .brown sweaters
    .brown scarves
   .velcro shoes soaking wet
   .green and orange together
    .firsts
.snow days
   .grapes in to-go boxes
   .crunchy snow
   .putting off homework to write lists
.middle school-esque crushes
.packages from home
.daydreaming

As a 19-year-old maybe I will....
move
get a cat
drop out of school
get a job off campus
finally get that big haircut
go vegan
be in a relationship ...or maybe not
question my identity
join that collective venue i'm curious about
change my major
gain more perspective
fully support myself
get a tattoo

02/10/04

I had a really great birthday. i'm 19. that sounds old.
this time next year i will be 20. 20!

friday night, daniel, hermonie (our newest friend from school),
and i went to a show at the talking head. it reminded me a lot
of shows in michigan. i guess because since i've been here, I've
mostly been to hardcore shows. but this one was an indie
show. they were all female-fronted bands, and the show was
a part of a weekend event called Gender Fest, 'celebrating
women in punk rock.' i turned 19 while i was at the show and
daniel and hermonie and i were sort of counting down and it
was fun and they sang me happy birthday. It felt like the
perfect place to turn a year older in a new city, especially
now that I'm more conscious of my place in punk.

i woke up saturday morning to my friends coming into my
bedroom singing happy birthday and all wearing fake braids
made of yarn and glasses which was really cute and funny,
and they made pancakes and gave me presents. Later that
night we all went ice-skating at the rink on the harbor with
the city lights as our backdrop. Then we came home late, read
zines, and we had a big sleepover with 8 of us all on the floor
of my living room under and over lots of blankets, and we
slept in our undies. it was very fun. we didn't actually sleep
until about 4. that was my birthday. I'm really lucky to have
found this group of people and to have started out with such
a great college experience. Some of my friends from home
are having a harder time finding their place.

ways to know you're hiding your
    feelings (from yourself & others)
    february 14, 2004

.you can't speak clearly about how
        you feel
.you're evasive
.you shut off your emotions
.you're confused
.you make others confused
.your real life and daydreams are very
        different when they could be
        equivalent.
.you contradict yourself

                -i have never-
    ----
    done any drugs

    been drunk

    had a long-term relationship

    traveled out of north america

    had sex

    danced at a dance

things i'm trying to stop doing
february 15, 2004

.whistling constantly
(i do it without even realizing it)

.making fun of people as the way i joke
around because sometimes they take me
seiously and then i'm a jerk

.using swear words other than
 'asshole' and 'dammit'

.censoring my feelings from myself
 and others

.being so blunt and honest
    (i guess that's more censoring though)

.wasting so much money on diet coke.

i just got photos back from the night that daniel got hit by that guitar. the photo is brutal! this is my best friend in the whole universe. he has a bloody head. we're going to get married i think. we waited in the hospital for five hours because of this.

he's a lot less bloody now and a lot more stitched up and way more hardcore. i know i said i like nice boys but this is pretty tough. swoon.

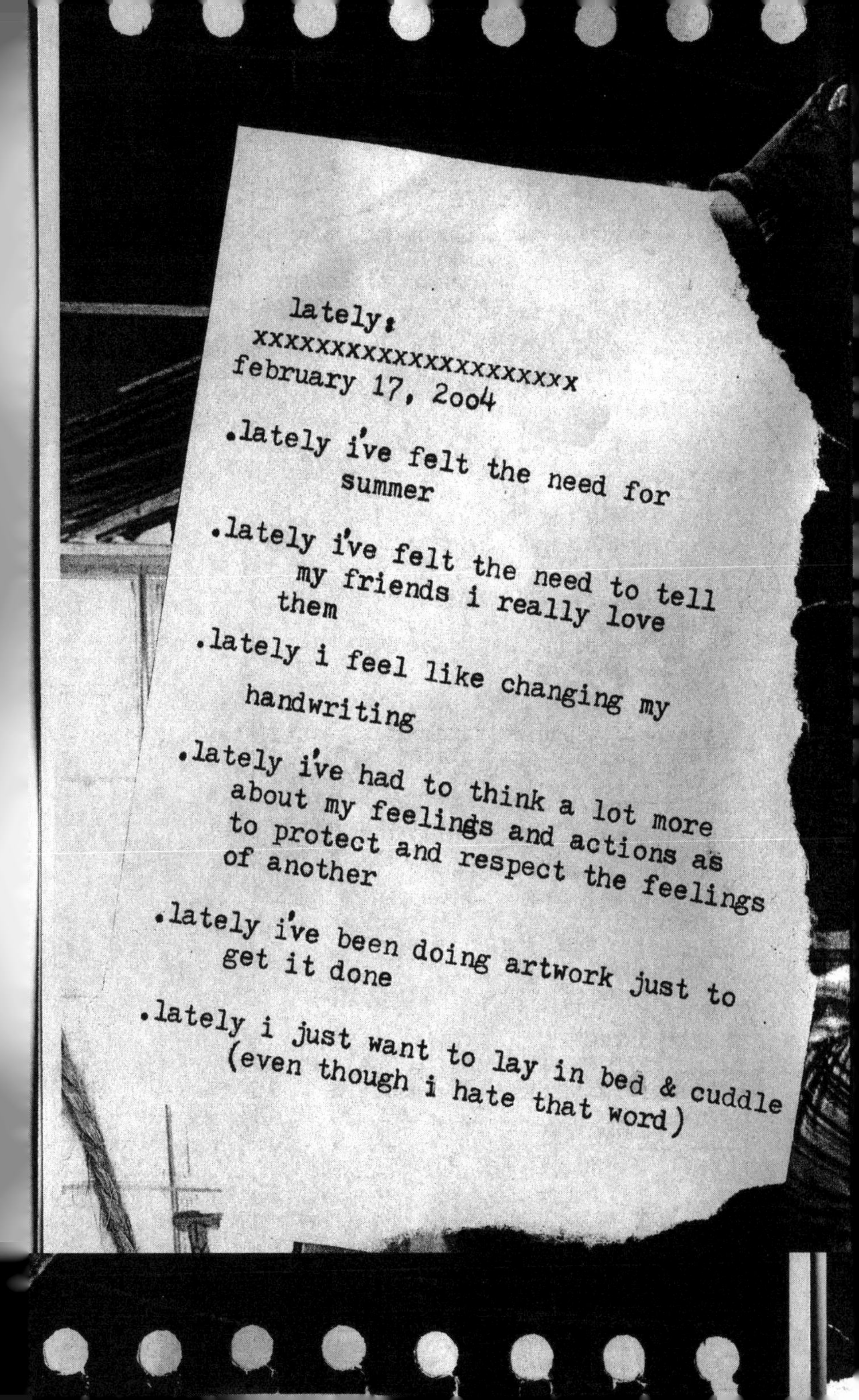

lately:
xxxxxxxxxxxxxxxxxxxxx
february 17, 2004

- lately i've felt the need for summer
- lately i've felt the need to tell my friends i really love them
- lately i feel like changing my handwriting
- lately i've had to think a lot more about my feelings and actions as to protect and respect the feelings of another
- lately i've been doing artwork just to get it done
- lately i just want to lay in bed & cuddle (even though i hate that word)

2/20/04

so hi. this week i found the most amazing perfect found list for my zine. it is entitled "things that taste blue." i feel like someone planted that list there just for me to find because it's too perfect.

the weather is so great lately. i can't get enough. i want to swallow big gulps of air and eat it all in its entirety. i miss the smell of lake though. the smell of lake in the springtime in michigan is so prominent. in michigan, apparently, you're never more than 5 minutes away from a body of water. maybe that's a myth but it's what i've always heard.

i hate that in not understanding my own feelings, i make someone else's feelings go all weird and confused. i wish our feelings weren't directly correlated because then i could be confused and not have to feel bad about it. sometimes writing letters to people you have strong or confused emotions about, knowing that you will never ever send the letter, is the perfect remedy to cure confusion. i think i need to write someone tonight.

i want michigan and break.

i need concrete feelings that i'm sure of.

why i like animation
and might change my major

-i like to make representational work
and to tell stories about myself (and hear
stories about others). animation would be
a good medium for autobiography

-it's something i've never done before and
this would be the perfect opportunity to
learn it
-it's an opportunity to learn a lot of
different skills under one umbrella: computer
animation programs, lighting, set-building,
sound design, film editing, storyboarding,
character design/illustration, etc

-it doesn't come with the same implied
pretension that fine art does. i just can't
take that attitude seriously...

-it's fun

-it would be a nice change of pace from my
years of art classes where i do figure
drawing, gestures, formal studies, etc

-we watch a lot of cartoons in class

-but we watch a lot of incredible films, too

-i'm pretty sure im gonna go for it...

                    summer, come sooner

-warm weather every day
-no homework!
-friends from home
-lakes and fields and woods
-endless nights driving around with friends
-hopefully working at the art camp i used
 to attend (i applied. just waiting to hear
 back! fingers crossed.)

-so much free time
-sleeping in
-sunshine
-roadtrips (daniel only lives two hours away!)

-swimming

-carefree all the time

-tans and sunburns
-grass in my toes
-change of pace that will make me appreciate
 baltimore that much more when i get back to
 it for my sophomore year, where i'll live
in an apartment with my friends.

things i do that people probably
              d o n' t k n o w

write letters to people that
i know i'll never send

match my underwear to my shirt

wear little boy undies

sing loudly to music in my car

wear the same pair of pants every
day

play the piano

daydream about you when you're
standing next to me.

look into people's windows from
far away

check my livejournal every
five minutes

come up with lists in my head that
i'll never write down

organize the shirts in my closet by
color and hang them on
appropriately colored hangers

goals - 2/26/04

1. finish the second issue of my
   zine before spring break. it's a
   zine filled with lists, surprise, surprise!
2. meet new people
3. continue to do situps every morning
4. make my drawing teacher like me. she's convinced
   i'm not passionate about anything. she almost
   has me believing it myself...
5. buy lots of records
6. quit living in daydreams when i could easily
   make my daydreams a reality. im just a wuss.
7. ??? . dont let thursdays make my head explode.

thursdays explode my head. they're so long. i stacked
two studio classes in one day. i like having a 4-day
weekend as a result, but having 12 hrs of class in one
day is so much. but, really, it's only so much right in
between classes when i've just had 6 hrs of drawing,
and i'd be home and relaxed at this point on a normal
day. but instead, i have to rush off to 6 more hours of
animation before i can breathe again and hang out and
put off homework.

:::sick:::

eyes itch
        hot

    head pound
        throat closed

        dizzy

hot faced

    achy joints
        cant breathe

pain
        out of focus
    zoned out

my downfalls.

.i procrastinate
.always think i'm right
.am too laidback
.fall for people too easily
.never let myself get close
.too opinionated
.too hard on myself
.lack good hygiene
.slack off
.am obsessed with the internet
.think too much
.am too easily amused
.let messes build up
.don't earn money
.take things for granted
.am too hopeful
.overextend myself
.leave myself open to be hurt
.trust too easily
.don't forgive and forget
.gossip too much
.don't take risks
.am too set in my ways

2/28/04

hi. i haven't seen nat in days. i haven't seen cory in days. i've seen ben a little more lately, but far less than i used to see him. it's pretty depressing. our big group is all in sections now, especially as people start relationships. but i'm overly happy with my daniel and hermonie subsection. we've been having a lot of fun.

we had a zine-making party earlier, and my second issue of my zine is almost ready to be photocopied. the rest of today is for homework on the roof. because homework under sunshine with a view of the city with music through headphones is the epitome of spring.

lately i've been craving home and summer, but yesterday, out of nowhere, i started to think about summer and became really sad because i can't imagine my life for 3 months without these people. that is such a long time. and i'm just warming up to people in certain ways and i like how things are going. and soon it will end.

Hey!
Daniel stopped by. I think he left some-thing for you.
a burned CD with one love song on it.
listen to the words
a funny and flirty list written by Daniel

things ramsey is mean to daniel
about... (daniel)
-------------------------------------- -

.hating everything

.being pants conscious

.dwelling and obsessing about
    things

.being hardcore

.thinking i'm smarter than other
    people

.being an activist about everything

.vegan

.having a hateful tone of voice

.being ugly

.being really ugly

.saying no to his hot date offers

.being ugly

THE END

p.s. being smelly
    having scummy hair

3/1/04

this weekend we had a sleepover on our roof because
the weather was beautiful (eventually it got really
cold though and our feet were all about to fall off)
but it was fun. sleeping next to certain people is really
nice, and i should try to do it more often.

3/5/04

today i was having a bad day. my drawing teacher almost has me believing that i don't care about any-thing. because that's what she thinks about me. she really puts me in a negative mood for the rest of my thursday. my past thursdays when i felt exhausted between classes? nope. i realized i've just been mad and that's really why my brain feels like exploding. i get that she's trying to push me, but not everyone thinks like she does and that should be okay.

things with friends have been weird. it's been hard as people couple off and start to hang out on their own. we don't really feel like a group anymore. after dinner today all i wanted was to go home. i just need a break, and i need to see friends on a positive note and not have to worry and feel negative. leaving sounds really nice. spring break is only in a couple weeks. i need it.

Do you see this inch? This one right here?
I want to see every inch like this from now on. This is the one moment of urgency I've seen from you. I don't care that you can render well.
Yeah.
That means nothing to me.
I feel like nothing I show her will be good enough.
Show me that you feel something.
You have such a wall around yourself.

if everyone was honest and good-hearted
we could...

.loan each other things without fear of never
  seeing them again
.travel easily without metal detectors, visas, or
  passports.
.barter and trade instead of relying on money
.have good middle school experiences
.not have to worry about being cheated on or
  stabbed in the back
.we could get naked without feeling self-conscious
.we wouldn't have to suspiciously peer over our
  shoulder as we walk alone at night
.we'd be less nervous speaking in front of crowds
.collectives would be the most common form of
  work environment
.we'd feel that our vote actually counts
.we'd be a lot more carefree

art school is weird

-weird sculptures all over campus

   -lots of nudity and sexuality

-pseudo shock value

  -huge installations

   -spending hours on tedious projects

 -wearable art

   -edible art

  -implied pretention

    -hip kids that intimidate me and annoy
    me all at once

-being totally desensitized to staring
at nude figures, sometimes ones that
have rat tail mullets

   -keeping myself awake for 48 hours and
   documenting my sleep deprivation

-watching cartoons for class

-people crying in class often, because
theyre upset at critiques or because
their work is really personal or powerful

-lots of weird clothes, weird hair, and
  weird antics

spring

3/12/04

spring break, now that I'm out of workstudy, is finally here and it's a relief. no thinking about deadlines or assignments for a whole week. phew. however, now that i think about it, a week is nothing. it's almost unsatisfying. like a little tease, but i'll take what i can get.

daniel and i are great.
sleeping in a bed alone for all of spring break will be a little bit weird after the past week or two since we've started really "hanging out." it feels right, the way we are now.

i just got off of work and i'm bored already. people don't hang out anymore. daniel and i just do because everyone else is hanging out in couples. but daniel is gone already in chicago for break because his fridays are free.

spring break will be good. several good shows, my favorite coffee shop, chicago, friends! my dog, all good things for one week.

3/22/04

this break was so busy and full and good

-big house show at my dad's house. 130 kids and
 money raised for a memorial fund for someone my
 younger brother went to school with
-25 person post-show late-night dinner
-bonfire at my friend ryan's house, laughing, crazy
 truck driving through a cornfield over jumps,
 group sing-alongs to johnny cash
-family dinner to celebrate mine and my mom's birthday (since i was gone last month for mine)
-show at the rocketstar, lots of dancing
-playing ddr in my basement with my little brother
-movies and music at merry's with all the girls
-dominic's birthday
-playing an open mic night with my band
-lunch with dad
-going to a show in chicago and seeing erins dorm
 and meeting her new college friends
-visiting daniel and meeting his family, watching
 his band practice, going to a show at the fireside
 bowl
-seeing daniel's band play a show
-saw my crush mx from last summer
-wandering around the mall with merry, katie, and fran
-more movies in merry's basement

break is done now! i'm all packed and very happy
with how i spent my break and who i spent it with,
and how everything turned out and is turning out.

now back to school, classes, and routine, but that's
okay because there's only a month and a half left
(that's really scary actually!). i don't know how
i'll feel about leaving my college friends for three
months, and if i work at my art camp, then i won't
have summer at home with home friends either.

but for now, i know i feel happy.

3/30/04

Things just are:

good.   getting better.

cuddly.   laughy.

full of procrastination.   lazy.

different.   not friend-oriented.

not what i'm used to.   weirdly balanced.

i have to start registering for classes soon. as an
'experimental animation' major (something i had never even
considering majoring in until i decided my favorite thing is
learning something entirely new and that I should do that
instead of just sticking with painting). i am excited but all
the course titles sound intimidating. i hope i still have time
to paint. this summer i will paint.
we sign the lease and pay first month's rent on thursday,
which means we get the keys to our apartment, which
means – sleepover! we went to see our apartment again
this weekend. It's going to be really fun living there with
my good friends.

the main source of my happiness right now? daniel and his
cute face and how dorky he is.

RELATIONSHIPS ARE WEIRD

-being in a new relationship makes me
feel weirdly vulnerable, even if it"s
with the person i considered a best
friend last week. why does the title
make me more nervous?

-i keep being afraid that i"ll do or
say something wrong that would make
him not want to date anymore. i guess
that feeling will go away after a little
while...at least i hope?

-we mostly just do all the same things we
did before we were "in a relationship."
why is it even necessary to have a label?
what does that change?i like the label,
but i don't really even know why!

-i'm kind of annoyed that my friends
in relationships just hang out as
couples all the time - but i can
already feel me and daniel doing that
a little. i hope it doesn't annoy
other people.

-does everyone else question things this
much, or am i a weirdo? i"ve never really
cared about relationships before. i've
never had a "real" boyfriend even,
because it didn't interest me. but,
daniel does interest me so i guess
that's what matters.

things i do with him
-act silly, wrestle, tease each other
-work on projects
-collaborate
-listen to records
-ride bikes late at night
-cook meals
-lay around and talk about everything
-learn and discuss

-sit at coffee shops
-read and draw comics
-read and write zines
-go to shows

-sit by the waterfront in the harbor
-dread a summer apart
-make each other mix cds
-eat a lot of food
-just have fun

one month left

-register for classes for next semester -
as an animation major!!

-get keys to our new apartment

-daniel's birthday

-fill out paperwork to work at the art camp

-pack up everything

-move what i can to our new apartment, take
everything else back to michigan

-slave over finals

-finish one more issue of my zine - i'm obsessed!
this one is going to have comics in it, which
is my newfound love thanks to stuff that
daniel showed me

-go to a few more shows in baltimore

-cruise around the city and enjoy it now that
it's warm out again. the city has come alive!

-cuddle a lot, don't think about the fact that
i won't see daniel much this summer... i hope
things don't just fizzle out...

-say goodbye to everyone.

-roller coasters
-critiques from my drawing teacher
-not knowing what the future holds
-moving in with all my best friends. hopefully
 we all get along in close quarters!
-being an animation major
-not knowing whether i'll be able to make
 a living as an artist or not
-not knowing what will happen with me and
 daniel if we take a summer apart right after
 things were just getting good
-political conversations, because they always get
 heated and go in circles, and i still don't feel
 like i can fully defend myself
-the upcoming election later this year
-walking alone at night in baltimore
-public speaking
-daniel going to protests a lot. he's an instigator.
-not having much money and having a tight budget
 all the time
-not exercising ever, now that i don't play hockey.
 this is the first time i haven't played a sport in
     seven years. i feel myself getting out of
     shape.

-being more on my own next year. fewer visits
 home, living off campus, taking classes of my
 choosing, etc.

things i'm going to
miss when the school
.......year ends..........
april 20, 2oo4.

.brick sidewalks
-most people here
.the food staff guy that sings
-the anticipation of checking
the package list
.hermonie
-riding the lightrail
-my friends
-having an accessible fire
escape and rooftop

things i collect

-ticket stubs
-photo booth pictures
-typewriters
-letters
-found objects
-bouncy balls
-set lists
-fortune cookie fortunes
-notes and tiny things
people do for me that
i think are special

4/25/04

Daniel is the best. I really like him a lot. He always makes me smile, and we have fun together, and he's just cute and nice to everyone. I'm appreciating him more and more every day. I've now had a real 'boyfriend' for a little over a month, an amazing feat for me. No negative thoughts of any kind. Usually, I talk myself out of being in relationships pretty fast. I never had a real boyfriend in high school even.

I'm getting a little excited about working at art camp this summer, but at the same time, I'm sad about going home. Lots of mixed feelings. Sad about not being with home friends all summer since I'll be working, sad about not being with school friends for a whole summer, but excited to be in a totally different role at art camp, counselor vs. camper. It'll be interesting to see how the two sides differ. It always seemed like the counselors had so much fun together. I'll be making money and get to help kids and be in an art environment. It seems like the perfect work situation for me, even though it means being out of town for two months straight. I can't work at my dad's office my whole life (which is what I did all through high school). This summer will be weird.

-nice weather
-vintage roller skates purchased at the thrift store
-finishing the third issue of my zine. i made
   45 copies to leave around campus and mail off
   to friends
-classes coming to an end
   -anything and pretty much everything
      involving daniel
   -talking with friends in a big group.
      reminiscing about the good times we've had
      over the year

-late-night pasta
-a hardcore show being held on campus, funded
   by a school club
-daniel and i cutting each other's hair
-a pretty great crit on my drawing final
-thunderstorms
   -sweet furniture at our new apartment, courtesy
      of cory's family who drove down with it
-red-and-white raincoats
-getting all my finals finished
   -icee pops
-seeing michigan friends in one week

not-so-good things about lately

-having to leave everyone here
-too much work for finals
   -running out of meals on my food plan
-having to clean a lot for move-out
   -thinking about not seeing daniel for 3 months
   -undecorating my bedroom

the good list is so much longer than the
bad one. i guess i'm mostly very happy.

can't wait for next year

- living in an apartment with friends
- learning something totally new and being
  able to draw comics for homework
- turning my zine into a comic zine
- living one block away from daniel

- getting a job off campus and having
  more money

- getting more involved with the baltimore
  punk scene

- feeling more at home in the city
- hopefully still being with daniel and
  having a good, supportive relationship
- learning more about activism and trying to
  get more involved with cool things in the
  city that i believe in

- just feeling more on top of things and
  more involved in general

traditions that i'll miss

-watching *The O.C.* together every week

-planning elaborate birthday parties for one another and always having them early in the morning for some reason

-saturday chinese food binges from "eat must be first"

-calling each other before going to the cafeteria so that we can all eat together

-late-night snack food runs to the convenience store

-homework parties

things that happened freshman year
that i didn't expect.

-ended up choosing a different major than
 i had planned. that's pretty big!

-i became more interested in politics and
 activism. i started out pretty apathetic.

-i didn't really change my appearance at all

-i felt pretty torn about art school in
 general. not about me doing art, but about
 being at an institution for it. there were
 a lot of things i didn't like about the
 structure, and the students, and bureaucracy

-i was a lot more homesick than i expected

-met someone i was really interested in and
 actually acted on it and let myself get close
 to them. usually i let things fizzle out as a
 crush, or at most, a fling.

-moved totally away from fine art and into
 the realm of storytelling and illustration.

-had a pretty easy time adjusting

just getting started

(or: things i think i'll learn when i get
back)

-still have so much to explore in this city.
 i can't wait to feel like i know all of
 its secrets. baltimore is the kind
 of place that takes a little while
 to really know and love.

-the world of animation, comics and
narrative storytelling. i had no idea i
would be into this stuff, and i can't wait
to start learning more about it and
 telling my own stories. i'm terrible
 at drawing comics even though i'm
 good at observational drawing.
 making stuff up is hard! i'm excited
 to get better.

-living in an apartment with friends for
 the first time. its going to be so much
 fun.

-continuing to build my relationship with
 daniel and figuring out how to make
 something like this last, because i
 really want it to.

-continuing to figure out how to be on
 my own, i need to reevaluate myself and
 my personality, and learn everything i
 can.

5/10/04

hi. i'm home. we were chased all the way home by lots of heavy thunderstorms but it was kind of fun and the trip didn't take too long. it was nice to talk to my mom and, once home, i was excitedly greeted by my dog and a record that had come mail-order for me.

i unpacked for as long as i could stand the harassment my dog was giving me for not immediately playing with him, and then i caved in, and we ran outside and played frisbee just as it started to downpour. as i was running around barefoot in long grass and pouring rain, playing frisbee with my dog, i remembered why i should be excited to come home. living in the city is nice but living in the country is simple and innocent, and you don't have to be afraid to hang around outside at night, and there isn't concrete everywhere, and it's just familiar and fun.
but i miss daniel already so much i think i'm going to explode. and now i need to unpack some more and find some friends to hang out with. This summer will be interesting. I feel like a totally new person trying to fit back into my old-person world.
I hope all my school friends have a good summer. i cant wait to see everyone again (already, haha)